PLANNING

Category: Business & Economics

Description: To get big results set big goals and make detailed plans. You will become a perfect example of a well organized sales professional. Every detail of every sales call will be planned out well in advance. At any given moment during the day you will be able to look at your schedule and be right on track. Benjamin Franklin's 13-week self improvement program will guarantee your success.

Key words: sales planning, territory planning, territory sales plan, territory management, territory management plan, territory plan, sales plan examples, sample sales plan, sales business plan, 90-day sales plan

Copyright Bob Oros-2017

ISBN 978-1-105-22259-7

Written and published by Bob Oros

PLANNING 1

Planning

To get big results make big plans

Lack of what skill causes 78% of sales people to fail?

When asking that question to a group of sales people the answers are all over the board. Closing usually comes out as number one, objections are number two, after that it is a toss-up between making presentations, getting people's attention, follow up and asking questions. The reason 78% of all sales people fail, or fail to reach their sales objective, is due to a lack of planning. At first this may seem a little off balance, however when you take a look at what planning really is, it takes on a new meaning.

For example, let's take a look at closing. The best time to think about your close is when you are planning the call. Instead of taking in one product to show your customer, take in three different quality levels. Instead of asking if they want to buy your product or not, you can

5

now ask them which product would best fit their needs. That is the choice close at its best.

Objections are another example. If we wait until we are in the buyer's office and he or she says "your price is out of line" it is a little late to start figuring out what to say. You know the objections you run into, and again, the best time to overcome them is when you are planning the call.

Let's take a look at making the presentation. There are very few products on the market today that cannot be duplicated, turning them into a commodity. Why should a customer switch to your product when the features and benefits are the same? Once again the time to find the "points of difference" that will make a professional presentation is during your planning stages.

How about getting the customer's attention? The average buyer is interrupted every eight minutes. If they have been buying for any length of time they have "heard it all." What are you going to do or say during the first 60 seconds that will make the customer lean forward and say "tell me more." If you are trying to think of something while waiting your turn to see the buyer, well, you get the point.

The old days of "hitting the street and making some calls" are pretty much in the past. Twenty years ago there was believed to be such a thing as a "Born Sales Person." Today you have to sell with "Surgical Precision."

Remove the "uncertainty"

How would you like to have an insurance policy that was going to guarantee your success in sales? I have that policy for you. It will guarantee success and remove all the "uncertainty" about selling.

Here it is.

The next time you become jittery because selling is such a risky business, consider this: The risk that an insurance company takes on one individual policyholder is the most unpredictable thing in the world.

What could be more risky than trying to guess when one certain individual is going to have an accident or become sick, or how long he or she is going to live?

Yet the insurance business itself is the most stable in the country, the safest investment anyone can make-the nearest thing to a "sure thing" in the way of guaranteed returns to investors.

The risk an insurance company takes on one individual policyholder is tremendous, yet the risk involved in 100,000 policyholders is so predictable it can be figured to the fourth decimal point.

Whether or not you will sell any single prospect is unpredictable.

But do as the insurance companies do; "spread the risk" by making a sufficient number of presentations.

By making a certain number of presentations you can adopt the attitude that "I've got nothing to lose" before making a call, instead of telling yourself, "Everything depends on this," you can now tell yourself that "EVERYTHING DOES NOT DEPEND ON THIS".

You can strike out occasionally and still hit more home runs than anyone else on the team. Say to yourself, "If I don't call on this customer and ask for the order, the sale is lost anyway. If I call on him or her and fail, I won't be any worse off than I am right now, so I have nothing to lose."

When you strike out a few times and keep going you get over the "fear of failure." Spread the risk like the insurance companies do, broaden your customer base and make more contacts.

How many customers do you need?

For many sales people marketing seems to be a separate division of the company with its own, unrelated agenda. However, marketing strategies can be used individually to help build your business.

The first step in marketing is to identify your target customer and determine how many customers it will take to maintain your business. Here's what I mean, using examples from different industries.

Let's say you wanted to sell residential real estate for a living. You would need to stake out an area that has a minimum of 500 houses. If you began a systematic schedule of contacting these 500 homeowners on a monthly basis, some in person, some on the phone, some by mail, there would be enough houses bought and sold each year to make a living.

Another good example is insurance. You would have to have a list of one thousand households and contact them on a regular basis. There would be enough insurance needs to earn a living. Both examples depend, of course, on your ability to out sell the competition.

Even a nursing home with one hundred beds has to have them filled with residents. If they have ten empty beds for any length of time their expenses go up and their profits go down.

A hospital is in a similar situation. The success of their marketing is measured by their "occupancy rate". The next time you call on a hospital ask what their occupancy rate is and you will be surprised at how quickly they can give you the percentage.

A manufacturer looking for national distribution needs 200 distributors. Fifty for each quarter of the country. This will result in enough coverage to sell in every corner of the US.

Looking at a restaurant's business from a marketing perspective can also be measured with mathematical precision. A restaurant needing to sell a thousand meals each week to take in enough money to pay all their expenses needs a customer base of five thousand. A marketing "rule of thumb" for a restaurant is to take one week's business and multiply it times five. Restaurant customers normally rotate their eating out, so you would want to be sure that you had five thousand people "rotating" into your business at least once every five weeks.

What about a Distributor Sales Rep (DSR)? How many customers do they need and how much do they have to sell each customer to make a living?

The average DSR sells a little over two million dollars each year, or $40,000 each week. The average order size is $500. That means to be "average" you would have to sell 80 accounts $500 every week. NOT A GOOD PLAN!

What if you double the order size to $1,000? That brings the number of accounts down to 40. Forty accounts purchasing $1,000 each week sounds better, however, you are still only "average".

Let's give it one more twist. Let's weed out the low margin price shoppers and carefully select 40 accounts that could buy at least $2,000 per week from you. Now you are investing your time and effort with prospects that will give you sales exceeding four million dollars per year.

It look's good on paper, as all marketing plans do. However, it is still up to you to make it happen the old fashioned way, by selling.

Write your orders in advance

Is it possible to write your orders in advance? What if you show up on your customer's doorstep with the order all made out and all you need is their signature? I would say it would be possible if the order was already placed, or they had called in and wanted you to stop by and pick up the actual order confirmation.

But what if it was a mistake? What if you made the call and expected to get the order, only to find out that they never called in? What if it was a set up?

I have to plead guilty.

I once conducted a test at a distributor to see if the sales person could get a better response when they believed they were going to make a sale verses calling on a customer without this belief.

On Monday the sales manager and I carefully selected 10 prospects, each in a different sales area that was not currently buying. In each account we obtained the name of the person who was responsible for doing the purchasing. Tuesday this information was passed along to the sales person in that area saying that the prospects had called in and wanted to talk to someone about placing an order.

This changed the dynamics of the entire call. Was there any hesitation about making the call? None. Was there any doubt about whether they might or might not want to see you? None. Was there a lot of time spent worrying about what to talk about. No. It was as simple as going to the store and buying a loaf of bread.

At the Friday sales meeting we confessed. After the dust settled, the results were discussed with each sales person. Seven out of the ten reported a positive response. They each admitted the call was made with a totally different frame of mind. There was no hesitation before the actual confusion started and obvious misunderstanding.

The lesson learned from this exercise was simple. If you know what you want, take action and expect to get it your results will be much better. And just how do you accomplish that? Make a plan for each call.

Planning your day or week

Planning is one of the most important activities of a sales person.

Winston Churchill was once asked how long it would take him to prepare for a 10 minute speech. He said he would like at least a month's notice. When asked how far in advance for a one hour speech he said at least a week, and when asked how long he needed to prepare for a four hour talk he said he could start now. He made an excellent point for planning presentations. To make an effective 10 minute presentation takes careful planning and organizing. If you were going to spend five hours with a customer it would not be necessary to spend a lot of preparation time because everything you want to discuss will come out in the course of four or five hours.

A successful sales person will spend one hour in planning time for each day of selling. It takes that much time to write letters, make appointments, prepare presentations and carefully think about the details of each call you are going to make.

What is the one tool all top sales people use?

An airplane is off course 97% of the time. The pilot carefully writes his or her flight plan with the destination and time it will take. Then the GPS system keeps correcting its course to stay heading in the right direction.

You have to continually monitor your progress to make sure you are on course, or in case you have to change and adjust your plan. An airplane flying from Chicago to NY may be off course as much as 97% of the time, however the pilot keeps adjusting and making corrections.

Selling is unlike many other professions in that you have to keep yourself motivated and organized on a daily basis. Many other types of work are built on the routine of doing something over and over again; however, selling requires a review of your battle plan every day. You have your over all objectives as well as the accounts you must see on any given week, but as you begin each day you have new situations and opportunities that did not exist yesterday.

The most important thing you can do at the end of each day is make a list of the things you have to do tomorrow and number them in the order of importance. Things may come up to change your program; however, a numbered list will give you a track to run on and will keep you working on the most important things first. The most important thing is to do it at the end of each day. If you wait until morning you may forget an important item. Also by doing it at the end of the day your subconscious mind will have a chance to work on your list during the night.

What's the point?

You can't do anything about the economy. You can't do anything about the new trends that are taking place in nearly every business. And there is very little you can do about customers shopping for bargains.

So what is the answer? What should you do to keep your business growing, or keep your business from going backwards? Who would have thought that we would get excited if sales were flat?

Here is the answer.

Since you can't do anything about the economy, trends, or customers buying on price, you should focus on what you CAN do something about. You CAN improve your skills. Those people in sales who think they don't need any training are the ones feeling the heat. The ones who never pick up a book, never listen to an audio CD and think that attending a seminar is a waste of time.

However, if you are reading this, you are not one of those people.

Let's see how good of a sales person you really are. Let's see if you can make a sale to yourself. Let's see if you can design and present a plan to yourself that will get you excited about sales in spite of what everyone is saying about the economy.

Here is a common mistake most people make when they lay out a plan for themselves, which you may be guilty of as well. You have been focusing on the FEATURES when you set your goals and make your plans. The FEATURES are boring. The FEATURES will never get you excited about your goals. You have to give yourself a BENEFIT presentation!

In case you are not clear on the difference between a FEATURE and a BENEFIT, a feature is a fact about the product or service, a benefit is what it does.

For example the feature of a Ford Truck is that it has a V10 450 horse power engine. The benefit is that it will pull a 10,000 pound trailer up a steep hill with ease. The BENEFIT is SEEING yourself driving the truck and pulling your RV or boat up the hill without any trouble. You don't sit around and admire the engine! And if you do, you are admiring the POWER to get the job done!

Here is another example.

I sell sales improvement seminars. Most sales people would rather have a root canal than attend a sales training session (that's why I call it sales improvement). Sales training is the FEATURE. The BENEFITS of my programs are more sales, more profits, new accounts, better contracts, more customers, more productivity, better territory management, and improved relationships - all resulting in growth. (If these things are important to you contact me and let's do something about the things we CAN DO SOMETHING ABOUT).

Personal goal setting is important. A personal goal is the only thing that gets you up and out the door early. It is the thing that makes you do things you normally don't want to do. However, what is even more important are the BENEFITS you will personally receive once your objectives are reached.

Here is another mistake most people make. It is easy to mistake a benefit of reaching a goal as the goal itself.

Here's what I mean. The down payment on a new house is not a goal; it is the benefit of reaching your sales objective. The extra money you want to put in your retirement account is not a goal; it is the benefit of reaching your sales objective.

You talk to your customers about the benefits of your products and services - why not make the same case for selling yourself on giving it all you've got?

Lack of goal setting is rarely a problem. You either set them yourself, or your company sets them for you. Goals in themselves rarely have enough power to motivate you to a high degree.

What will motivate you are the personal BENEFITS from accomplishing your goal. Your goal as a sales person is simple: Exceed your sales plan.

Exceeding your sales plan is a FEATURE not a BENEFIT. The achievement of this goal is assured the moment you commit yourself to it. How many benefits will you receive when you exceed your sales objective?

Once the benefits are listed, you will find the personal motivation that gets you out the door early. The motivation to overcome call reluctance. The motivation to make the extra call. The motivation to ask for the additional business.

Your single goal is to exceed your sales plan. Stop now. Take out a piece of paper. Make a list of the BENEFITS you will enjoy by exceeding your sales plan. List all the BENEFITS you will receive once you exceed this goal. Better yet, get some pictures that represent the benefits and picture yourself as already having achieved them. If you can't think of any, get some pictures of Maui and plan on taking your family to the best vacation spot in the world, or somewhere you would really like to go.

Growth is the purpose of life. If you are not growing you are simply taking up space in your current position. You have to grow until you become larger than your current position. If you are new it will take three years of intense study and consistently making calls to really become successful in sales. And even then, you have to keep growing personally and learning new skills.

This attitude of GROWTH in a sales person is imperative. You MUST have it. You MUST want more. You MUST be aggressive with your actions and demand a lot from yourself. If you don't feel that way, do yourself a favor. Go to work in another profession.

Your built in GPS

As I write this I am in Columbus Ohio and just took my rental car back. I didn't have to worry about how to find my way around because I had a GPS (Global Positioning System) telling me where to go. All I had to do was put in my destination and, like magic, I was given step by step detailed instructions on where to go.

Here's what I was thinking. "Wouldn't it be great if I had a GPS that would guide me towards my goal? I could program in my goal and get minute to minute feedback telling me if I am on course, or if I need to change direction or change my activities."

Well, you guessed it.

You and I do have a GPS already installed. It just has to be programmed. Once you enter your destination you will be guided with surgical precision. Here is the biggest problem with our GPS. We don't have confidence that it will actually work. We seem to have more confidence in a GPS that is placed on the dashboard than the one place between our ears!

So the first part of the programming process is to choose a specific destination. It has to be specific. You can't program a GPS to head south. You have to enter an address, or at least a city. It can't be a destination that is unreachable or unclear.

The input must be realistic, measurable, obtainable and most important, specific. You have either reached your destination, or you have not. There is no gray area. As soon as you reach it you can enter your next destination.

And be sure to program your GPS with ACTIVITY goals. You will never know if you will sell any single person, so the goal of "open 2 new accounts" will never work. Instead program the activities it will take to get 2 new accounts. "Carefully select 10 new prospects and start contacting them every week until 2 or more place an order." Your GPS will respond without any problem.

Your GPS will let you know if you are off course by planting some guilt and self doubt if you DON'T keep your promise to yourself. It becomes easier to make the 10 extra calls than to keep hearing your GPS in the background telling you that you are a loser! (That's part of your guidance system). If you MAKE the 10 extra calls your confidence and self esteem will be higher. (Also part of your guidance system).

It makes sense that if you don't know what you want to go, or what you want to accomplish, you won't ever establish a working plan of action. The purpose of the GPS is to keep bringing you back on track. Everyday things happen to really mess up the plan. But with your GPS destination you keep coming back on track.

You have to keep entering your GPS data! According to everything I have ever read about goal setting it all seems to communicate this message: You have to rewrite your goal every day. So it is like a GPS. Every morning sit down and write your goal and your list. Your built is GPS will be working in the background to get you there.

Without a goal it is like a trip I took to Quebec. Everything was in French. Everything! I couldn't read a single road sign. Had I not had my GPS I would have been completely lost. However, all I had to do was enter the address of the hotel I was heading to and presto, step by step instructions were given to me.

So... what is the address you want to end up at? Write it down. Give you mind a clear picture of what it looks like and presto! Step by step instructions will come to you almost like magic.

Sales clerk or sales professional

When someone brings up the topic of a sales person what is the first thing that comes to mind? Most likely it is a well dressed man or woman with a smile and an extended hand ready to give you that warm friendly greeting.

You may think of a real estate sales person who is eagerly showing you a house, a car sales person demonstrating the features of a new automobile, or a foodservice sales professional sitting at a table in a restaurant making a presentation to a chef.

That is all part of the selling process, but just about anybody can do that with a little training. That is only 20% of what it takes to be a real sales professional. So what is the REAL job of sales?

I am going to give you a crystal clear picture of what selling really is. And once you understand it you will be able to focus on that single area and your business will take off.

For example let's look at a car sales person. When someone walks into the dealership they have already decided they are going to buy a car. 80% of the sales process is done for them! All they have to do is help the person who has already decided to buy a car, decide which model to buy!

Let's take away the showroom. Let's take away all the hundreds of thousands of dollars spent on television, radio and newspaper advertising. Let's put the cars in a warehouse where the only way to see one is by making an appointment with a sales person. Let's have the car sales person work out of his or her home. And let's say that the only way someone could find out about a new model is from a sales person telling them about it.

Now we are on an even playing field. Now there is no showroom where they meet every morning and WAIT for the hundreds of thousands of dollars spent on advertising to kick-in and bring someone in to look at a car. The car dealer and car manufacturer have done 80% of the work a real sales person would have to do, find prospects.

Now, let's say you are going to sell cars without all this help from the company. You are sitting at home by yourself trying to figure out who might be in the market for a car. You have no massive marketing campaign, no showroom, no leads that your company provides for you, no one calling you up asking for information about a car. You have to make it all happen by yourself.

And that is the heart of selling.

Prospecting. Finding customers who are interested in what you are selling. Getting people to stop what they are doing and listen to your story. Knocking on doors. Getting referrals.

A real sales person has to eat what they kill.

A "sales clerk" (someone who has 80% of their sales job done for them) eats what someone else has killed.

A real sales "professional" knows the truth. When YOU think of sales you know what it feels like to be sitting in a fast food restaurant, discouraged because it seems hopeless. You know what it feels like to be turned down over and over again. You know how difficult it is to boost your attitude back up after losing a customer who "decided to go in a different direction!" You know how difficult it is when you lose a customer to a competitor. You know the TRUTH about what selling REALLY is.

To really be successful in sales you have to be able to plan. I mean really plan! I mean sit down and ask yourself some tough questions. Where am I going? Who am I going to call on? Why should they listen to me? How can I prove that they will be better off with me rather than what they are currently doing? How many calls do I have to make to get a new customer? How can I find all these prospects I need?

What does your week look like? What kind of tracking system do you have to keep all your contacts in order? How many times do you follow up with a prospect before you write them off? How many cold calls do you have to make to land one new sale or one new client? How do you qualify your prospect as someone worth calling on? Once you get them in the pipeline what is the process you use to keep bringing them to the "next step?"

You can't really call yourself a "sales professional" unless you have to scrape up your own leads, plan your day, follow up and keep your sales funnel full of opportunities.

If you simply go into the office, showroom or store and wait for someone to come in and buy something, sorry, you are a sales clerk. You still have to learn a certain set of skills to help people decide which one to buy, or to explain the features and benefits of a product they already have an interest in.

But that is a lot different than walking into a prospect's business or office and talking with a person who is perfectly happy with what they are doing and has no interest in making any changes. Getting their interest, getting them to a "next step" in the sales process, getting them to agree to a demonstration, getting them to pull out their checkbook. THAT is what a professional sales person does.

And THAT takes a highly organized plan. Spend whatever time it takes to make a detailed plan for the week and you will be doing what the 78% of sales people who fail don't do! Why? Because they have this incorrect picture of what selling really is.

So get this picture right. Being a sales professional is the very heart of any business. Be proud of the fact that you can keep going, keep picking up the phone and calling, keep knocking on doors, keep dealing with some really rude people who treat you like a doormat. And be proud of the fact that you can still come home to your family at night never giving a hint about how tough it is to be in sales.

If you are a "sales clerk" you can easily be replaced. Why? Because the company does all the work for you. As a "sales professional" you know how to plan your work and generate sales. You never have to worry about being unemployed because you are the most valuable person on the planet. Never forget that. And never stop improving your skills and conditioning your attitude. Always be on the offensive. Always be looking for new customers. Always be looking for new ideas. Always have an attitude of service. Always be willing to do whatever it takes.

To walk out the door of your home every morning without an office to hang out in, without a showroom to give the false sense that you are actually working, without a store full of products, that is what it really means to be a sales professional. Without a plan you will join the ranks of the 78% of sales people who fail.

Establish a goal

What do you want? Are you looking for financial security, professional acknowledgment, spiritual attainment? Do you want to fit better socially, or become more expressive creatively? Establish the goal that's right for you.

Then turn that goal from a dream into a desire. You want to realize that goal, not just wish for it. Aesop said, "Beware that you do not lose the substance by grabbing at the shadow." Know exactly what you want, then go for it.

Don't be tricked by your own procrastination - especially if you want to achieve something artistic. The writer

Thomas Wolfe wrote, "I had been sustained by that delightful illusion of success which we all have when we dream about the books we are going to write instead of actually doing them. Now I was face to face with it, and suddenly I realized that I had committed my life and my integrity so irrevocably to this struggle that I must conquer now or be destroyed."

Can you see what you want? If you want the abundance of material wealth that money provides, what goal will give you that money? Do you want the prestige of owning your own business? What business do you want to begin?

Where are the opportunities for you? Talk to everyone in the business you want to join. Make friends in the literary or art societies in your area. Read books and articles about your field of endeavor. How can you attain your goal?

"If you don't want to work, you have to work to earn enough money so that you don't have to work," wrote Ogden Nash. And isn't that the way" Money makes money; success breeds success. But not always. How can you break through those thoughts to help yourself to the rewards?

Henry David Thoreau wrote, "I have learned this at least by my experiment: that if you advance confidently in the direction of your dreams, and endeavor to live the life which you imagine, you will meet with success."

Set big goals and visualize success. Do you see yourself in a big house? Maybe you picture your artwork hanging in a gallery. Can you feel your book in print and in your hands? How does it feel to be a person of success? Believe that you are; believe that it is in your grasp. That's what the others did, and that's how people make it to the top.

Then get down to basics. Be precise. Exactly how much money do you want, and by what date? And exactly what are you going to do to earn that money? Be realistic, but give yourself short-term goals.

Write it down. In six months or one year, you will have how much money. And repeat it until it feels good. Then repeat it twice a day until it swirls in your subconscious, until it becomes your one-pointed goal

Planning: To get big results make big plans

I am a perfect example of a well organized sales professional. Every detail of every sales call is planned out well in advance. At any given moment during the day I can look at my schedule, at my list of things-to-do and be right on track. Everything I do is completed step-by-step in perfect order. I spend whatever time it takes to work out the details of every sales call I am going to make during the week. Not simply an itinerary, but everything I want to accomplish with each customer. My customers are always amazed and impressed with the amount of thought and preparation I put into every sales call.

My 4% improvement objective:

_____

_____

_____

_____

_____

_____

About the author Bob Oros (BobOros.com)

The principles in the book series were uncovered the old fashioned way: Hard work. Personal interviews with 507 professional buyers and 3,759 company owners were conducted to uncover the REASONS WHY they bought from certain sales people, or what they did to get a sales person to lower their prices. The information was then tested online by 4,838 new and veteran sales people from all 50 states and six continents to prove these findings would produce results. Since then the principles have been presented in seminars and workshops more than 2000 times for some of the largest companies in the country.

What the entire course will do for you

Buying all 13 books is like buying a library of 13 powerful coaching sessions that will increase every skill necessary for generating business. Once you experience the seemingly effortless improvement you will understand why there is a picture of Ben Franklin on every 100 dollar bill.

You will learn how to improve relationships, improve management skills, be more productive, generate more customers, negotiate better contracts, open new accounts, earn more profits and create more sales! Results most people only dream about! If you are a sales professional or an entrepreneur this is the perfect program to boost your sales and increase your profits.

Ben Franklin's system

In our fast paced business and personal life today it has become increasingly difficult to set aside time for self development and improving your skills. With every spare minute taken up by reading blogs, logging on to Facebook, following people on Twitter, responding to text messages and emails and constantly talking on your cell phone, there seems to be little, if any, time left for learning new skills. Even the quiet time behind the wheel of your car is no longer available with satellite radio and cell phone coverage in every corner of the country.

Even though this seems like a new problem, distractions have been around forever. Two hundred years ago a man by the name of Ben Franklin had the same problem. He concluded that it was not a matter of distractions as much as a matter of focus. He set out to solve the problem and created the most effective system for self improvement ever invented.

Ben Franklin gives credit for all his success and accomplishments to the implementation of this system for the success he sought after. Despite being born into a poor family and only receiving two years of formal schooling, Ben Franklin became a successful printer, scientist, musician, author and one of the founding fathers of the United States. Ben Franklin is considered to have been one of the most persuasive and successful people in the history of the United States. He was a very skilled sales person, marketer, negotiator and copywriter. Skills that every business owner, professional person, manager and marketer should have.

In the year 1723, Ben Franklin, at the age of seventeen, arrived in Philadelphia without a penny to his name. At age 42, he retired, wealthy, the first self made millionaire in the country. Few people, before or since have ever been as successful as Benjamin Franklin. He gave credit for his many inventions and business successes to his system for self improvement he created when he was 20 years old.

The key to Franklin's success was his drive to constantly improve himself and accomplish his ambitions. In order to accomplish his goal, Franklin developed and committed himself to a personal improvement program that consisted of mastering 13 principles.

When he was seventy-nine years old, Benjamin Franklin wrote more about this idea than anything else that ever happened to him in his entire life. He felt that he owed all his success and happiness to this one thing. Franklin wrote: "I hope, therefore, that some of my descendants may follow the example and reap the benefit."

Since success is developed by performing small and seemingly insignificant acts, you can use this method by reading and putting into practice the 13 skills that will guarantee your success in sales with scientific certainty.

This program takes advantage of Franklin's system and applies it to improving your skills as a sales professional. This program will show you how to dominate your market by first dominating yourself. By focusing on the 13 skills that make up a highly effective and successful sales professional. As these skills are improved your results and sales increases will also show a dramatic improvement.

The goal of going through the program the first time is to increase each skill by only four percent. With the accomplishment of this small improvement in each skill or attitude your overall improvement will be 52%. Those are results most people only dream about. However, you can accomplish this by investing as little as 45 minutes once a week reading one book and then focusing on improving the single skill during the rest of the week. The second week by reading the second book and focusing on that single skill during the week and so on until all 13 weeks are completed.

You can write the single word on the back of your business card and tape it to your dash board as a reminder. You can put this one word on your smart phone as a reminder as well as on your email signature, your Facebook page or you can even have something worthwhile to tweet about. One word, one week, one skill, one "I am" statement, 4% improvement objective and your subconscious mind will receive the message through all the clutter and act on it.

After the first time through the process you can do as Ben Franklin suggests and go through the program a second, third and fourth time. Get your whole sales team on the same page at the same time and you will experience a whirlwind of new excitement and new business. Or get a like minded colleague and join forces with accountability and focus.

Achieve a 52% improvement

Using Franklin's scientific program for learning your objective is to improve 4% in each area over 13 weeks.

1. Attitude Define what you want and go after it.
2. Respect Earn respect-no more comfort zone.
3. Service Help customers build their business.
4. Urgency Be enthusiastic get things done now.
5. Confidence Remove restrictions and limitations.
6. Persistence Keep going and never give up.
7. Planning Get big results by setting big goals.
8. Questions Ask questions that make the sale.
9. Attention Get attention with irresistible offers.
10. Presenting Give reasons why they should buy.
11. Objections Remove every roadblock to the sale.
12. Closing Ask for the order and get paid.
13. Follow up Remove all hope for competitors.

About the author Bob Oros (BobOros.com),

Bob Oros has been a full time speaker and author since 1992 with over 2,000 speaking engagements in all 50 states and several international locations as well as the author of 21 books on sales. Prior to starting his speaking career, Bob served six years in the US Navy as a Communications Specialist and then worked his way from a street sales person to the position of National Sales Manager for a Fortune 200 company.

CSP Award: Bob was awarded the designation of Certified Speaking Professional (CSP) by the National Speakers Association and the International Federation for Professional Speakers. Fewer than 10% of all speakers worldwide qualify for this award.

PWA Member: Bob is a member of the Professional Writers Alliance.